A BICYCLE
COUNTRY

BY NILO CRUZ

Play File Bicycle
Cruz, Nilo.
A bicycle country /
c2004.

A BICYCLE COUNTRY
Copyright © 2004, Nilo Cruz

All Rights Reserved

CAUTION: Professionals and amateurs are hereby warned that performance of A BICYCLE COUNTRY is subject to payment of a royalty. It is fully protected under the copyright laws of the United States of America, and of all countries covered by the International Copyright Union (including the Dominion of Canada and the rest of the British Commonwealth), and of all countries covered by the Pan-American Copyright Convention, the Universal Copyright Convention, the Berne Convention, and of all countries with which the United States has reciprocal copyright relations. All rights, including professional/amateur stage rights, motion picture, recitation, lecturing, public reading, radio broadcasting, television, video or sound recording, all other forms of mechanical or electronic reproduction, such as CD-ROM, CD-I, DVD, information storage and retrieval systems and photocopying, and the rights of translation into foreign languages, are strictly reserved. Particular emphasis is placed upon the matter of readings, permission for which must be secured from the Author's agent in writing.

The English language stock and amateur stage performance rights in the United States, its territories, possessions and Canada for A BICYCLE COUNTRY are controlled exclusively by DRAMATISTS PLAY SERVICE, INC., 440 Park Avenue South, New York, NY 10016. No professional or nonprofessional performance of the Play may be given without obtaining in advance the written permission of DRAMATISTS PLAY SERVICE, INC., and paying the requisite fee.

Inquiries concerning all other rights should be addressed to Peregrine Whittlesey Agency, 345 East 80th Street, New York, NY 10021. Attn: Peregrine Whittlesey.

SPECIAL NOTE

Anyone receiving permission to produce A BICYCLE COUNTRY is required to give credit to the Author as sole and exclusive Author of the Play on the title page of all programs distributed in connection with performances of the Play and in all instances in which the title of the Play appears for purposes of advertising, publicizing or otherwise exploiting the Play and/or a production thereof. The name of the Author must appear on a separate line, in which no other name appears, immediately beneath the title and in size of type equal to 50% of the size of the largest, most prominent letter used for the title of the Play. No person, firm or entity may receive credit larger or more prominent than that accorded the Author. The following acknowledgments must appear on the title page in all programs distributed in connection with performances of the Play:

A Bicycle Country was commissioned
by the Joseph Papp Public Theater,
George C. Wolfe, Producer.

It was first produced by Florida Stage,
Louis Tyrrell, Producing Director;
Nancy Barnett, Managing Director.

SPECIAL NOTE ON SONGS AND RECORDINGS

For performances of copyrighted songs, arrangements or recordings mentioned in this Play, the permission of the copyright owner(s) must be obtained. Other songs, arrangements or recordings may be substituted provided permission from the copyright owner(s) of such songs, arrangements or recordings is obtained; or songs, arrangements or recordings in the public domain may be substituted.

A BICYCLE COUNTRY was produced by Florida Stage (Louis Tyrrell, Producing Director; Nancy Barnett, Managing Director) in Manalapan, Florida, opening on December 10, 1999. It was directed by Benny Sato Ambush; the set design was by Kent Goetz; the costume design was by Lynda Peto; the lighting design was by Jim Fulton; and the production stage manager was Suzanne Clement Jones. The cast was as follows:

JULIO .... Gilbert Cruz
INES .... Sol Miranda
PEPE .... Oscar Riba

CHARACTERS

JULIO, a man in his 40s

INES, a woman in her 30s

PEPE, a man in his 30s

TIME

Before the U.S. intervention on Cuban rafters.

THE SET

The set is a square platform with a column in the middle. To the right of the column there is an old trunk and two wooden chairs. The wooden platform becomes a raft in the second act. Objects needed in the play are taken out of the trunk or the characters bring them in from the offstage area. A white cloth or screen on the upstage area frames the stage. A large round orange spotlight is reflected on the white drop for the day scenes and a large round white light for the night scenes. The white screen can also change in colors according to the mood of the scenes. For the last scene the white screen or cloth should open or drop, to reveal a green landscape.

A BICYCLE COUNTRY

TIERRA

ACT ONE

Scene 1

Projected on the screen: TIERRA. Music plays. Julio is standing, strapped to a wooden board with a rope. The board leans against a column. Ines stands close to him. She writes a few of Julio's instructions on a small paper. Pepe sits at the table.

JULIO. I don't have an alarm clock. My eyes open at seven o'clock. That's the time I wake up.
    The first thing you give me are the pills. They are right here by the night table —
PEPE. He takes one of the pink ones, two of the yellow. Right, Julio? After he takes the pills you give him —
JULIO. After I take the pills, she gives me the bedpan.
PEPE. Yes ... It's under the bed.
JULIO. I take two to five minutes on it. Sometimes more.
PEPE. *(Trying to ease the situation.)* That's a good time for you to occupy yourself doing something else. You can smoke a cigarette —
JULIO. No. She goes to the kitchen to heat up the water for my bath.
PEPE. Yeah, you go to the kitchen —
JULIO. At seven-ten I should be ready. She takes the bedpan and cleans me. When she finishes cleaning me, she gets rid of what's inside the pan. Then she goes to the kitchen to get the bucket of water for my bath, and she comes back to me — That's around seven-fourteen ...

PEPE. Seven-nothing, Julio! ... *(To Ines.)* I'll instruct you as you go along. Don't worry. I'll teach you.
JULIO. I want to be dressed by seven-thirty, and that is our goal.
PEPE. Yeah, no shoes till he's ready to stand.
JULIO. *(Looks down at his feet.)* I have to get used to the standing position. It's good for my circulation. We do this twice a day, when I get up in the morning and an hour before I go to sleep. What time is it now?
INES. It's almost nine. At what time do you go to sleep?
JULIO. Sometimes nine ... Sometimes eleven. It depends ...
INES. What do I have to do to help you?
JULIO. Well, there are things that have to be done before I go to sleep. It's part of the nightly routine. Please, unstrap me. I'm ready to go to bed. *(Ines unstraps him. She places her right shoulder under his arm to help him sit in a wheelchair.)* I'll sit here for a bit to catch my breath.
You can go to the kitchen and heat up some milk. I drink a glass of warm milk before I go to bed.
INES. You won't fall?
JULIO. I can hold myself up.
INES. *(To Pepe.)* Would you help me in the kitchen? Show me where everything is kept.
PEPE. Sure. *(Ines and Pepe move toward the kitchen.)*
INES. Pepe, I want to talk to you.
PEPE. What's the matter?
INES. You didn't tell me ... You didn't tell me everything had to be so ... I don't know ... So, paranh, pin, punh ... So by the clock. *(Julio wheels himself close to them to hear the conversation.)*
PEPE. I told you he likes things done a certain way ...
INES. He's like a commander. I don't know if I can work under these conditions. I don't know if I can. I worked in a hospital, but I don't know if ...
PEPE. He's a good man. You have to get —
JULIO. *(In a loud voice.)* Pepe ...
PEPE. He's calling me. *(In a loud voice.)* Coming ... *(Walks to Julio.)*
JULIO. Is she all right?
PEPE. Yes ... I mean ... No. I think you're scaring her away.
JULIO. *(In a loud voice.)* Ines.
INES. *(Joining them.)* Yes.
JULIO. *(To Pepe.)* Why don't you explain to her that it takes time

6

getting me dressed?
PEPE. I've helped him —
JULIO. *(Interrupting him.)* Why don't you explain to her, that if she follows my instructions we can make more use of time?
PEPE. He says —
INES. I heard.
JULIO. Explain to her that if she follows my method —
PEPE. You see, it takes time getting him up from —
INES. I understand.
PEPE. *(To Ines.)* It's different when you can't do things on your own.
INES. How much is he going to pay me?
PEPE. Julio.
JULIO. Half of what I'll receive every month.
PEPE. He's going to get money for being on relief.
He hasn't gotten it yet.
INES. So, how does he expect me to start working, when he doesn't have any money?
PEPE. Julio.
JULIO. Pepe, come here. Come close. *(Julio whispers something in his ear. Pepe nods. Julio unclasps a gold chain from around his neck. He takes the chain and gives it to Ines.)*
INES. What's this for?
JULIO. Your first salary. That's your pay.
INES. I'm not taking his chain.
JULIO. Why not? You can sell it or trade it for something.
PEPE. You see, he's paying you already. You can start working.
INES. No, give it back to him. He can pay me when he gets his money.
Tell me what else needs to be done.
PEPE. He listens to the radio before he goes to sleep.
And you have to give him one of the yellow pills.
INES. You'll have to excuse me I want to change my shoes.
These shoes bother me.
JULIO. You should make yourself at home. You can take off your shoes if you like.
INES. No, thank you. I don't like to walk barefoot. *(Lights change.)*

Scene 2

Projected on the screen: A MONTH LATER. Julio is sitting in his wheelchair exercising. He lifts his arms up and down. Ines helps him with his right arm.

JULIO. That was twenty.
INES. Again.
JULIO. That was twenty-one.
INES. Again!
JULIO. Twenty-two.
INES. More!
JULIO. Twenty-three.
INES. Two more.
JULIO. I can't.
INES. You want to get better!
JULIO. I can't anymore!
INES. One more time.
JULIO. Twenty-four.
INES. Come on ... You're strong.
JULIO. That's twenty-five ...
INES. One more. Try again.
JULIO. That's it! No more!
INES. You can't rest now.
JULIO. You're killing me!
INES. You'll go to waste if you don't exercise.
JULIO. I can't do all the repetitions.
INES. To say I can't is to say I won't do it.
JULIO. It's too much.
INES. You want me to blow some air on your face? Are you fatigued?
JULIO. We're done for today.
INES. No. You have to do more.
JULIO. You're out of your mind. What do you think I am, an athlete?! I'm sick!
INES. You're better than you think you are.
JULIO. You're not inside my body! I hurt.
INES. I'm just here to help you. If you don't want to do anything

for yourself, then stay the way you are. I'm going outside, it's hot in here. *(Starts to exit.)*
JULIO. No. Wait!
INES. What?
JULIO. What are we going to do next?
INES. Walk.
JULIO. *(Moves away.)* No walking. I told you I'm not walking.
INES. You walked yesterday after the exercises.
JULIO. I can't today.
INES. Then I'm going outside to smoke!
JULIO. Ey, don't get angry!
INES. I just want your cooperation.
JULIO. I don't like pain. My whole body aches.
INES. It's going to hurt. What do you expect? You don't use your muscles. They're flaccid.
JULIO. I need nutrition. I need to get stronger. It takes time for the body to heal.
INES. Of course, I know that.
JULIO. So, it's not going to happen overnight! *(Pepe rides his bicycle. He rings the bell.)*
INES. That's Pepe with the mail. *(Pepe parks the bicycle.)*
Come in, Pepe.
PEPE. Good morning!
INES. Good morning.
JULIO. Morning.
PEPE. *(To Julio.)* You don't look good. *(To Ines.)* And you don't have a good face either. *(Puts his bag down.)* What's wrong?
INES. What do you think happens in this house every day! *(Turns to Julio.)*
JULIO. What do you mean? I don't always complain!
INES. You complain every day, Julio.
JULIO. I'm not an athlete.
    She makes me exercise as if I was training for a tournament.
INES. He's exaggerating.
JULIO. Explain to her ... Tell her how I was a month ago. How I had tubes coming out of my mouth and IVs in both arms.
PEPE. So now you're better. What's wrong with exercising?
JULIO. *(Moves away in the wheelchair.)* Ah, the hell with you! You're just like her.
INES. He's mad because I added five repetitions to his exercises.
JULIO. She says it like it's nothing.

PEPE. Why don't you try helping her out? Pretend you're training for a sport. Baseball. It's not any different. If you have to run five laps, you run the five laps. You condition your mind to do it.
JULIO. When I played sports I wasn't sick.
PEPE. Here, mail for you. *(Goes through a bundle of mail.)* You got a postcard from Venice. And you also got a letter from the Interior Ministry ...
INES. Don't give it to him now. I'll take it. *(Grabs the mail.)* He has to finish his exercises.
JULIO. Give me my mail! Let me see my postcard.
INES. Here. The rest stays with me. If it's bad news you'll get in a rotten mood, and you won't do anything else. *(Gives him the postcard.)* You still have to walk.
JULIO. What did she say?
PEPE. Come on, be a good sport. You have to cooperate. Be more hopeful, my friend.
JULIO. That's all I need hope. What can I hope for?
PEPE. That's unlike you. You've turned into a lazy animal.
INES. Yes he has. He's turned into a hippopotamus that wants to stay in the water and do nothing for himself — Don't look at me that way. I read a magazine article about the hippopotamus. *(Julio gives her a dirty look.)* The hippos don't want to evolve. The penguin is an evolving animal. Penguins want to move forward. They're up on their feet and walking about. The seals, too. Those are evolving animals. But hippos want to stay in the water and do nothing for themselves. Just like Julio.
JULIO. You like to bother me, don't you? You like to bother me.
INES. No. I'm just not going to move from here until you walk.
PEPE. And neither am I. *(There is a pause. Julio looks at them in disbelief.)*
INES. What are you doing on Sunday, Pepe? Do you want to go to the Botanical Gardens? *(Julio wheels himself to another part of the room.)*
PEPE. What's at the Botanical Garden?
INES. There's a flowering tree from India I want to see. I was reading about it in the newspaper. This tree lives for two hundred years. It grows and grows for all these years, then it blooms once in its lifetime and dies away.

It gives so many blooms that the weight of the flowers makes the tree bend down and fall to the ground.
PEPE. That sounds like a nice thing to do on Sunday, go see a tree.

JULIO. She also said, she wanted to talk to the tree, and sleep under it before it falls down. I have a lunatic in my house.

INES. So what's wrong with visiting a falling tree, Julio! I'm going outside to get the laundry, when I come back you'll take a walk. *(Ines starts to exit.)*

JULIO. Give me the rest of my mail ... Give me my mail ... *(Ines is gone now.)* She's not giving me my mail ... She's mad, crazy ...

PEPE. *(Walks in her direction. He contemplates her from a distance.)* She's beautiful. Passionate. I love her.

I remember the first day I saw her. She was trying to catch a canary that had gotten out of the cage. I just stood there and watched her make her way slowly to the bird, her hands full of seeds. After two minutes the bird couldn't resist her anymore and flew into her hands. Couldn't resist her, I tell you. I'd like to have a woman like her in my life.

JULIO. No you wouldn't. She's like a sergeant.

PEPE. Well, that's what you need. Somebody to get you back in shape.

JULIO. You're talking as if —

PEPE. Treat her well. You don't want to lose her.

We found the right person to take care of you. She's hard-working, kind and determined.

I'd marry her if I were in your shoes.

JULIO. What are you talking about? I'm a mess. Who's going to want to look at me in this condition?

PEPE. You never know. She's a good woman. I don't like to see you alone.

I'd like to see you get married again. You deserve someone like Ines. She's a giving person. Nowadays a person calculates what they can afford to give.

The world is changing, my friend. It's not how it used to be.

JULIO. Are you sure you're not the one who likes her?

PEPE. Me? Of course not! I can stay alone. I like my freedom. I like being alone.

JULIO. Have you tried getting back with Lolín?

PEPE. Lolín is gone, Julio. She's gone. She must be in America, for all I know. Got away on a raft. Didn't even say goodbye.

JULIO. Why not?

PEPE. Who knows with women! She wouldn't talk to me after we had that big fight.

JULIO. She probably thought you would turn her in for leaving

the country.
PEPE. *(With contained anger.)* Would I do that! Would I do something like that! *(Pause.)* Give me a cigarette, will you? You and I have rotten luck with women. *(Julio gives him a cigarette.)*
JULIO. When did she leave the country?
PEPE. I don't know, probably two or three weeks ago. I didn't know she had left. Somebody told me.
JULIO. You're not taking this well, are you?
PEPE. No, I'm not. It's pointless. Why don't we talk about you?
JULIO. I have nothing to say. I feel rotten, like always.
PEPE. We should've left this place long ago.

Look at the two of us, alone again.

It's getting tough out there. You don't know how bad it is, because you never leave the house. But I can tell you, we're slowly going back to the Iron Age. We're in the Bicycle Age out there. We've gone back to the wheel. A whole country riding bicycles. You only have to look outside the window and see for yourself. Everywhere signs, slogans: "Save energy. Save energy." What energy is there to be saved, when there is no energy!

No oil. Hardly any buses running. I think this is the worst it's gotten in years.

I mean last night the only thing I had to eat was an egg. I sat down to have dinner. I saw the miserable egg, in the middle of my plate looking at me, like an eyeball. The thing gave me the creeps. I mean it looked like it was hungrier than me.

Just didn't have dinner at all, ran out of the house, got on my bicycle and went for some fresh air. I could feel my adrenaline going through my veins and up to my mouth. I think that's what filled my stomach last night, my own fuckin' anguish frothing on my tongue.

— Do you know what I'm trying to do now? Did I tell you? I'm trying to learn Italian.
JULIO. Italian? Why do you want to learn Italian for?
PEPE. Sure. Why not? Learn a few words ...

I want to hook up with an Italian tourist.

Imagine if I find an Italian woman. That would be my ticket out of this country. I'll get married, she'll send for me ...
JULIO. Ah, give me a break. Do you really believe it's that easy?
PEPE. Why not? Even if I don't get to marry her, it's one way out of this mess.
JULIO. So who's teaching you Italian?

PEPE. Who's teaching me Italian, hunh?! Someone lent me this Italian sewing book. *(Takes out a small book from his pocket.)*
JULIO. A sewing book. And what are you going to learn with an Italian sewing book?
PEPE. Oh, you should've seen me carrying on a conversation. I went to a bar and found an Italian woman and I said ... Listen to this ... *(He flips through the book and finds a section. He enunciates every word with natural speed and mastery.)* "*Questa giacca é strappata, desidero che mi sia rammendata.*" Tell me if that doesn't sound good!
JULIO. What does it mean?
PEPE. Can you sew a button on this coat for me?
JULIO. You told her that!
PEPE. Doesn't it sound good? Listen to this ... "*Desidero che mi si prendano le misure per un abito.*" That means I want to be measured.
JULIO. You're out of your mind.
PEPE. Ey ... She thought it was amusing. I got her talking. I needed a punch line.
JULIO. Did she punch you back on the face?
PEPE. No. We had a good conversation. Then, she went to the bathroom, and I had three drinks waiting for her to come back.
JULIO. Did she come back?
PEPE. No. I spent all my money on drinks. Today I'm poor and shitting blood. I have an ulcer. I can't drink. *(Ines enters with a bundle of clothes wrapped in a white tablecloth. She places it on top of the table. She continues talking as she makes a couple of knots with the four corners of the tablecloth.)*
INES. Did you hear me from out there? I was calling you to come out onto the patio. There was a whole flock of birds flying over the house. Hundreds of them. You can tell the season is changing. You can tell by the birds, they come here for the winter, then start making their way back North.
   Are you almost ready, Julio? Have you had a chance to rest?
JULIO. I've already told you, it's enough for today.
INES. Did he tell you what the doctor said? *(There's silence.)*
PEPE. What's the matter, Julio?
INES. Julio, he's talking to you.
   (To Pepe.) Was he always like this?
PEPE. No. I don't know what's gotten into him. He was always well disposed.

JULIO. I have to have surgery. *(To Ines.)* Does that make you happy?
PEPE. What kind of surgery?
INES. I told him he should do it. It's the only way he's going to get cured.
JULIO. When I leave this place, I can have surgery. When I get my travel permit.
INES. When you get a travel permit! When you get a travel permit! You're going to have to wait a long time for a travel permit. You better find somebody with a boat and leave this place. If you wait too long, you're going to go pim, poom, right there and have another stroke!
JULIO. *(To Pepe.)* Pim, poom ... Everything is pim, poom to her! Everything happens in a matter of seconds.
INES. He could have another stroke, if he doesn't have surgery. That's what the doctor said.
JULIO. In her mind she has gotten a raft and sailed up North from this room.
PEPE. And why not, Julio?
INES. That's right. He knows he can't be waiting around.
   Do you know how long it takes to get a travel permit?
JULIO. And where am I going to get a boat?
INES. *(To Pepe.)* Can't you get somebody to build a raft? I told him I'll go with him.
   What's important is to go, leave this place.
PEPE. It's not impossible. We can get a raft.
JULIO. Then you two can get inside the raft because I'm not going anywhere. What if something happens, enh?
PEPE. Why do you always have to think of the worst!
JULIO. Because you only have to look at me sitting in this wheelchair! I can't do much for myself, goddamnit! I'm an invalid! *(There is a pause.)* — Come on, let's go. Let's go ... I'll take a walk.
INES. *(Tenderly.)* Good. That's a good sport.
   Pepe, as soon as I stand him up, you take the wheelchair and stand there where you are.
   Julio, you're going to walk to him.
JULIO. That's too far. Take two steps forward.
INES. *(To Pepe.)* You stay where you are.
   (To Julio.) Let's see, put your arms around me, as if we're going to dance.
PEPE. You want me to play music?
JULIO. Shut up will you! Don't be a clown. *(Julio stands up to*

walk. Pepe turns on the radio. A rumba plays.)
PEPE. Why not? You need something to liven you up.
INES. Don't drag your feet. Lift up your feet. *(Pepe moves the wheelchair out of Julio's reach and gets back to his place. Dialogue overlaps.)*
JULIO. I'm trying. Turn that shit off!
INES. Lift up your leg.
PEPE. That's it, Julio …
JULIO. Turn that shit off! It doesn't let me concentrate!
PEPE. Bravo Julio! Bravo! You're doing it!
INES. Push forward!
PEPE. Go Julio! Go! Walk! To the finish line …
JULIO. Tell him to shut up!
INES. Shut up! Can't you see he's concentrating.
JULIO. Just tell him to put the chair behind me.
INES. No. You walk all the way to him.
PEPE. Go Julio! Go!
JULIO. Bring the chair, big mouth!
INES. Don't do it, Pepe.
JULIO. Tell him to bring the chair.
INES. *(To Pepe.)* Let him finish turning around.
PEPE. That's it … That's it Julio. There you go. *(Ines lowers Julio down.)* Bravo Julio … Bravo … *(Pepe goes to turn off the radio.)*
INES. Are you all right? *(There is a pause. Julio catches his breath.)*
JULIO. You want me to throw myself to the sea — look at me! How can I put myself in a little raft, on a truck tire, when I can't walk well enough?

Can't you see I'm drowning! I'm sinking in my own body. I'm sitting here on solid ground and I'm drowning. *(Julio wheels himself out of the room. There is a pause. Ines looks at Pepe.)*
PEPE. *(Taking his bag.)* I'll come by later. *(He starts to exit.)*
INES. Pepe, what is this thing that he has that won't let him move forward? *(Lights change.)*

Scene 3

Projected on the screen: FIVE MONTHS LATER. Five months have passed since the start of the play. Ines gets a sheet. She drapes it around Julio. She gives him a photo album. She gets a pair of scissors and starts cutting his hair. Julio flips through the photo album.

INES. How long ago was that? You look young in that picture.
JULIO. I was seventeen.
INES. And this guy standing by the seawall?
JULIO. Guess?
INES. Pepe. But it doesn't look like him.
JULIO. He was probably twelve. Look at him in shorts. He used to love the sea.
INES. And that doesn't look like you either.
   You look handsome with that mustache. You should grow one.
JULIO. Let me look in the mirror. Let me see what you're doing.
INES. No. Not until I'm finished. I still have to cut your sideburns.
   Who are those people wearing sunglasses, in that picture?
JULIO. That's me and Ana Maria. She was feeding the pigeons in the park.
INES. Let me see. You still love this woman, don't you?
JULIO. That was the past.
INES. I know when she's on your mind. I've seen your eyes water.
   I know you well enough. I've worked in this house for five months now. The only thing left is to pin myself to your skin.
   Sometimes I feel like I am your body, and you are my brain.
JULIO. I don't want to talk about her.
INES. Then cut her out of your mind, like I cut your hair.
   She's not coming back, and thinking about her won't do any good. It's just like those pills you take, when you get depressed — she doesn't go away with pills. She left you. She could've taken care of you.
JULIO. Ines please …
INES. I just see you sad-eyed sometimes …
JULIO. Now come on, that's none of your business.
INES. You are my business. You're my work. That's why I come to

this house every morning.
JULIO. But we're not married.
INES. Ha! That I know.
JULIO. Good. Is that all you have to say?
INES. Yes.
JULIO. Then that's enough! Please, just get on with the haircut! *(She continues to cut his hair. There is silence. Pepe rings his bicycle bell.)*
JULIO. That must be Pepe with the mail. He'll cough now. He always does. *(Pepe coughs. Julio laughs. Ines chuckles.)*
PEPE. Good morning!
JULIO and INES. Morning …
PEPE. What are you two laughing about?
JULIO. I was telling Ines that I know when you're here by the cough. *(Pepe takes off his bag.)*
PEPE. Well, at least this ship won't get lost in the fog — It looks good Julio. *(To Ines.)* You do a good job. Can I be next?
JULIO. This is not a barbershop.
PEPE. She's good at it. I need a haircut.
INES. Today is Julio's birthday.
PEPE. I know. Happy birthday! Here. *(Throws him a pack of cigarettes.)* I got you a pack of French cigarettes for your birthday.
INES. I'm giving him my present later this afternoon. It's a surprise.
JULIO. Thank you, Pepe.
PEPE. How old are you? *(Ines undrapes Julio.)*
JULIO. Ancient. Old.
Let me look at myself in the mirror. Pass me the mirror.
INES. You stand up and get it.
JULIO. I guess no one is cordial anymore.
INES. That's right. We're mean and awful people. *(Julio gets up to get the mirror.)* See how well he's doing. See how good he looks.
PEPE. *(Applauds.)* Bravo, Julio … Bravo.
JULIO. I'm getting there.
INES. I told him we should go to the seawall and get some fresh air.
I told him we should have a party.
JULIO. That's for kids who like birthday parties. I'm too old to be celebrating my birthday.
(He takes a small lamp out of a trunk.) I want you to sell this lamp, Pepe.
I need money. I want to pay Ines.
INES. That's a beautiful lamp. You don't have to sell it to pay me.
PEPE. Aren't you getting paid at the end of the month?

JULIO. No more payments. They want me back at work. They say I'm capable of working at the office.

How much do you think we can get for it? *(He lights the lamp. The light reveals a painting on the lamp shade.)*

PEPE. I don't know. It's an old lamp. I can never estimate the price of old things.

INES. Don't sell it, Julio. Things get passed on in our families and we take them for granted. But these objects have a life. They become part of the family. They've lived with us.

JULIO. Like this lamp, Pepe, she's my cousin.

INES. I'm not saying anything else! It's your house, those are your objects ... You do what you want! *(To Pepe.)* He knows he doesn't have to pay me. I can get by until he gets back to work.

JULIO. *(He gives Pepe an old silver pot.)* Here. Take this too. How much can we get for this?

INES. That's silver. Don't sell that.

JULIO. I don't use it. How much?

PEPE. You won't get much money for it ... I could exchange it for food, a couple of chickens.

INES. Get a tire. Exchange everything for a tire. Let's build a raft and get out of this place! *(There is a pause. Julio stares at Ines. She was so direct in her response, it's as if her mind had spoken before she could come up with the words.)*

It's not going to get any better here. Every day more and more slogans. The permanent war: "Contribute" ... "Resistance" ... "Do It for Your Country" ...

Every day the same story, no room for questioning. They take away your food and they tell you: "Keep on going ... You can go on ... " Call *this* moving, call *it* going on.

The spirit of the system ... They take away the fuel, no more buses ... Now a bicycle, just ride it. Call it a bicycle to take you to the sea, fresh air ... That's it. You have adopted the right spirit towards things ...

Only one dress to wear, call it one dress for a year. A year for a dress ... A dress without a year. I'm tired of fooling myself.

— If you don't want to leave this place, I do! I do! You can give me a raft for payment! *(Silence. She doesn't know what else to say and Julio doesn't know how to respond.)*

I'm going outside for some fresh air. *(Pepe tries to make light of the whole situation. He drapes himself with the sheet. He sits on the chair. Ines starts to leave.)*

PEPE. Aren't you going to give me a haircut? *(Ines ignores him, she continues out.)* Does this mean she's not going to give me a haircut? What happened, Julio? Where is she going? *(In a loud voice.)* Eh, I'm ready for the haircut. *(To Julio.)* Is she coming back? *(In a loud voice.)* Ines ... Ines ... *(He goes out of the house, still draped in the sheet.)*
(Ines takes Pepe's bicycle.) Hey ... come back ... come back ... *(Pepe enters the house.)* She took my bicycle. *(Music plays. Lights change.)*

Scene 4

Projected on the screen: LATER IN THE EVENING. The men are waiting for Ines outside the house. Ines rides the bicycle. She rings the bell several times, expressing joy and excitement. She has a package.

INES. I'm back. I'm back ...
PEPE. I was getting worried. Next time tell me where you're going.
INES. I didn't take long. Come inside. Close your eyes, Julio.
JULIO. What for? What's this all about?
INES. Just close your eyes. I have a surprise for you. Come on ... come on ... Close your eyes. *(Julio closes his eyes. She leads him into the house. She places a box on his lap.)* Open your eyes. *(Julio opens the box. It's a radio.)* Yours doesn't work well and this one is portable. Now you can listen to the news all day. *(Kisses him on the forehead.)*
JULIO. Why did you do this? You don't have to give me a present.
INES. Happy birthday!
 Let's have a drink. *(Takes out a bottle of rum. Goes for three glasses and pours.)* Find a good station on the radio. We'll have to toast. Say something, Pepe.
PEPE. To ... To Julio del Valle. To many ... many more.
 That didn't sound good. I want to say something brilliant.
INES. To his health! And next year in another land.
PEPE. Yes, why not? All of us somewhere else. Somewhere else ... Good appetite! Isn't that what the French say?

19

INES. Something like that.
PEPE. Then grand, big, good appetite. Appetite to eat a whole cow to you, Julio. *(Toast.)*
JULIO. Salud ...
INES and PEPE. Salud ...
INES. We'll have to dance.
JULIO. No, no, no, no ...
INES. Come on and dance with me. *(Ines pulls his arm to dance.)*
JULIO. Dance with him.
INES. You have to dance.
JULIO. I can't dance. I don't know how to dance.
INES. Oh come on!
JULIO. No ... no dancing ...
INES. You're lying. You can dance.
JULIO. You're crazy. I don't want to dance.
INES. Well, I won't force you. I'll leave you alone because it's your birthday. *(Pause.)*
 I went real far to get this rum. I know this is the one you like. I wanted this day to be special.
JULIO. *(Pours more rum in her glass.)* You want more, Pepe?
PEPE. Sure. *(Toasting.)* "To your health! We would all like something better. Life is like that. We all want something better."
 See, I'm getting better at this. *(They drink.)*
INES. Play music, Pepe. We'll dance. Oh, I can feel the rum rising to my face. *(Pepe switches on the radio. An old bolero plays, maybe "Veinte Años."*)*
 Leave that song on! I love old music. I used to collect music like this one. Oh! I collected all kinds of things ...
 Oh! So many things gone. Got rid of everything ... All of it gone ... *(Dances by herself.)* Gave everything away ...
 I thought I was going to leave this place. But it never happened. *(The rum makes her giddy. She laughs.)*
 I was stupid. Gone mad in the head. And all for a German tourist. With him I went to all the nightclubs. I wore sunglasses and pretended to be a foreigner. All the waiters thought I was from Brazil, Italy, Portugal, until the German would get stuck ordering something, and I would have to open my mouth. *(She laughs at herself.)*
 He was gone at the end of summer ... August ... September ...

---

* See Special Note on Songs and Recordings on copyright page.

Gone away ... *(She becomes bitter.)* Like all foreigners, they leave when the seaweed comes to the shores. The scum of the sea. He left dressed the same way I met him, starched white shirt ... I stayed a mess, a shipwreck ... *(Determined.)* — Oh, I'd like to live in a place where the land extends and I can walk for miles, where I can run and never reach the end.

Here, there's always the sea. The jail of water. Stagnant. Just the sea — Oh, this rum is going to my head, Pepe. *(Ines stops dancing and goes to the table.)* Are you happy, Julio? Are you happy on your birthday?
JULIO. I'm as happy as can be.
INES. That's the most important thing, for you to be happy. Drink with me! Drink Pepe! Drink some more! *(She pours more rum in their glasses.)*
JULIO. No, that's too much.
PEPE. Drink up ... Drink up ...
INES. That's it drink ... Oh, I want to dance again. Let's dance.
PEPE. No. No dancing. No more dancing ... *(Switches off the radio.)*
JULIO. Let's just sit. Let's just sit and talk. *(The rum is loosening her spirit now. But she's not drunk.)*
INES. Can you drink a lot, Pepe? Can you drink a lot without getting drunk?
JULIO. Oh, he can drink like a fish.

I've seen him drunk more than a couple of times. *(Both men laugh.)*
INES. I can't drink. *(Lifts up her glass.)* It all goes to my head, it opens my mouth and I talk too much. That's why I never drink. We talk too much, period. We are too loud and loose with our tongues.
JULIO. And what's wrong with that? What's wrong with talking?
INES. We should measure our words, like the English.
PEPE. If I do that, then I wouldn't speak my mind. If you measure your words, then you don't really say what you feel inside.
INES. *(Sits down.)* I think the Germans are like the English. They can talk to you about their deepest sorrows and still keep their calm.

The German man, he was always talking about politics. He was always arguing whether we had gotten stuck because of the Americans or the Russians, whether we would survive all alone in the middle of the sea.
JULIO. Probably saw the worst year we had. The first year the Russians abandoned us ... We were all like ants, running here and

there. Wondering what would happen next.
INES. — Oh, I don't like talking about politics. To me wars seem useless and unreasonable. Destruction. God destroys, but his destruction is always justified. He destroys in perfect order. He's an artist at it. After his hurricanes and earthquakes, there's always a blue morning with clouds. And if there's rain, it's because he hasn't finished cleaning up after himself. But we haven't learned to master that art. Man is sloppy and messy and he can never master that art. *(There are tears in her eyes. She is lost in memory, her own destruction swelling in her throat.)* Oh, why couldn't I leave this place! What's the use of staying in one place for so long? *(She lowers her head to her arms. Julio looks at her full of love and affection as he reaches out to her. Pepe remains quiet and still. He looks at them. Lights change.)*

Scene 5

Projected on the screen: TEN DAYS AFTER JULIO'S BIRTHDAY, OCTOBER 11, 1993. Sound of rain and thunder. The stage is semi-lit. There are folded sheets and pillowcases on top of the table. Ines sits at the center of the table, mending a pillowcase. Julio stands next to her.

JULIO. Pepe came by late last night and I gave him a few things to sell. I gave him a vase and some old jewelry I had.
INES. You're selling everything, Julio. The house is starting to look sad.
JULIO. That's all right.
INES. You're not going to sell these, are you? I'm mending them.
JULIO. No. I did give him some more old frames and silverware. I told him to get what we need to go out to sea.
INES. Does this mean ... Oh Julio!
JULIO. Yes, I'm ready to do it. I'm ready to plunge myself into the sea. What do I have to lose?
INES. Oh, Julio! *(Embraces him.)* So? So?
JULIO. He's going to find somebody to build a raft.

INES. When is it going to be ready? When are we leaving?
JULIO. Calm down. We still have to find more things.
INES. Is Pepe coming?
JULIO. Yes he is.
INES. *(Hugs him.)* Oh, Julio ... *(There's an awkward moment when their bodies touch.)*
JULIO. Is there food?
INES. Yes. There's soup left from last night.
JULIO. Shouldn't we turn on the lights? You're going to hurt your eyes.
INES. It's not that bad, I can see. The rain brings a light of its own and I like sewing in this light. The rain makes me do things I don't normally do. It makes me sit down like an old woman and do this. Look at this pillowcase ... The string got pulled out, and you can't make out the initials. The D looks like a C backwards.
JULIO. All that linen is falling apart. They've been in the family for so long.
INES. I know it's old. But it's still beautiful.
  Who knows how many generations! How many heads have slept on this pillowcase. I was just imagining all the women in your family, who slept on this pillowcase.
  I like your last name. I've always liked last names that begin with the letter D: del Campo, del Valle, de las Casas, de los Angeles. It makes one's name seem more regal. It makes you feel as if you belong to something, of this, of that. It just flows like history.
  — I want to lay my head on this pillowcase. Close to you. *(Looks at him. They embrace.)* I love you, Julio. *(They embrace again.)*
  I want us to forget who we are. Start a new life away from here. Let's forget who we are. *(She kisses him on the forehead.)*
JULIO. *(She takes the pillowcase and gently tries to cover his face.)* What are you doing?
INES. A game. Just a game to start a new life. Just let me do it.
  Look at me. *(She takes another pillowcase and places it over her head.)* When we lift up the cloth we'll start a new life. (Music plays. Julio lets his face be covered by the pillowcase. Now she covers her own face with a pillowcase. He touches her face through the cloth. He brings her close to him. They kiss through the pillowcases. The sound of the sea fills the stage. Blackout.)*

End of Act One

AGUA

ACT TWO

Scene 1

Projected on the screen: AGUA: THE SEA. Blue lights. The sound of wind and sea fill the stage. On a raft in the middle of the Caribbean Sea, Ines and Pepe are rowing. Julio is standing, facing upstage with a compass in his hand.

PEPE. A good-for-nothing, I tell you. A miserable-wretched-mind-blind-deplorable beast. You can ask Julio what it took to get food, a piece of meat out of that moron.
JULIO. Yes, she was an imbecile.
PEPE. It took bidding didn't it?
JULIO. Persuasion, eh! The imbecile wouldn't take anything.
INES. This rowing is getting to me, Pepe.
PEPE. Don't think about it.
— I said to the mountain woman, "What does it take to do an exchange? You give me a few pounds of jerked beef and I give you this radio. Good condition. The radio plays music like an orchestra. Long antenna. Picks up northern stations at night ... western stations, eastern stations, as far as Vienna." I even told her that I had danced to Viennese waltzes at night, and all from the radio. And what did the moron say, Julio?
JULIO. "No. No love. No music."
INES. What did she mean by that?
JULIO. I said to her, "Love yes, much love. You sitting on a horse riding through the prairies, playing the radio."
PEPE. Yes, then he told her, "Jerked beef for us, radio for you ... Radio for love."
JULIO. Ines and the moron started to laugh, and she said, "Hee ... hee ... Love ... No love ... Hee ... hee ... A scratch ... A scratch in my heart ... My big sister stole my love."

PEPE. I felt sad when she said that …
JULIO. Let me finish, Pepe … She said, "Maybe radio for crying." But then she said, "No … No … If I cry, Mama will holler at me." That's when she told us to go to Adolfina, that she had fat chickens and lots of jerked beef.

Then I saw the mountain woman looking at Pepe's bicycle and I pulled him aside and told him, "I bet you anything that if you give her the bicycle, she'll give us the ten pounds of jerked beef." And wasn't I right?
PEPE. Yes, you were.
JULIO. I said to him, "Even if we have to walk ten miles, we're not going anywhere without getting the jerked beef."
INES. Is this it?
JULIO. Yes. We figured it's the only thing that wouldn't spoil.
PEPE. Do you think we're on the northeastern current? Roberto said that when we reach the straits of Florida, the currents flows eastward. Are we still moving towards the northeast?
JULIO. *(Looks at compass.)* If this compass is any good, it looks like we're moving north.

What does it look like to you?
PEPE. Yes we're moving northeast.
INES. Are you sure we're not moving towards the northwest?

Which way is east?
PEPE. *(Points to the left, then the right. Then makes up a new direction.)* This way. No, this way. This way. This thing can't make up its mind. It doesn't like pointing north now.
INES. I don't see the current moving us to the east or to the west. I just see waves. How can you tell the current is moving eastwards? How can you see in this darkness?
JULIO. The compass, Ines. The compass.
INES. I've been rowing for more than five hours and it feels like we haven't moved a bit. That thing doesn't work. Look at what happened to Columbus, he wanted to go to India and ended up in the Bahamas and Puerto Rico.
PEPE. We can't even see the city lights. Of course we're moving.
INES. *(Stands up and looks at the seascape.)* I can. I can still see the shimmering lights.
JULIO. Where?
INES. Back that way.
PEPE. That must be the reflection of the moon on the water.
INES. It feels as if we're inside the mouth of a wolf.

JULIO. A whale.
PEPE. *(Rowing.)* Let's get to it, Ines: One, two ... One, two ... *(Continues to count between the lines.)*
JULIO. Take a break.
PEPE. *(Rowing.)* We have to pass the picket line!
We have to pass the picket line!
INES. How do we know when we pass the picket line?
PEPE. There'll be ships, American coast guards. Balloons ...
INES. Will they be able to see us in the dark?
PEPE. There'll be thousands of ships, people waving at us. Come on, one, two ... one, two ... one, two ... one, two ...
INES. Take a break. I can't rest if I see you rowing. I start feeling guilty.
JULIO. Take a break!
PEPE. *(Stops rowing and lies back.)* Give me a cigarette, Julio.
INES. *(After a pause.)* I don't know about you but I'm afraid. I get this bad feeling in my heart. Ay, I start to think that we'll end up drowned!
PEPE and JULIO. Ines!
INES. *(Covers her ears.)* No ... I didn't say that. Tell me you didn't hear me say that. *(Uncovers her ears.)* But I had to say it.
JULIO. That's why we have to keep our minds away from those thoughts. We have to think about other things.
When I was in the military, one time we got lost — for days stranded in the wild, under the scorching sun. We just couldn't find our way back to camp. And I used to tell myself, We're getting there ... We're getting there. I'd repeat it over and over again in my mind. I would picture the city, the streets, the buildings and that's what kept me going.
INES. What we need is a nightcap, something to put us to sleep. I just never thought that water could be so frightening.
JULIO. It is frightening.
INES. All this darkness.
PEPE. I've never seen so many stars.
INES. And look at their reflection on the waves. You can't even tell if the stars belong to the night or the sea. It makes me want to fish them out of the water.
Give me something to drink, Julio.
JULIO. We have to save the water.
INES. I've been rowing for five hours I need some water.
PEPE. He's just trying to save the water. If we run out of water we're in bad shape. Remember what Robertico said, no matter

what happens we can't drink salt water.
JULIO. You guys are going to have to turn around. I have to take a leak.
INES. Yes, I've been wondering how I'm going to pee, because you guys can just pull out your thing. I'm afraid of sticking out my butt and getting bitten by a shark. I've seen a few circling us.
PEPE. So have I. I just didn't want to say anything. They've been following us for some time.
JULIO. So aren't you going to turn around? *(Pepe and Ines turn around. There is a pause.)*
INES. Well?
JULIO. Give me a second, will you!
INES. *(After a pause.)* Did you finish?
JULIO. I can't do it.
INES. How come?
JULIO. I can't pee when there are people around me. It takes me longer.
INES. You better get used to us.
PEPE. Listen to the water, it will make you want to pee.
INES. Pssssssssssssssssssssssssssssssssssssssssssss ...
JULIO. What are you doing?
INES. That's what my mother used to do when my brother couldn't pee.
JULIO. Forget it. I'll pee later.
INES. You better get used to us.
JULIO. I will. I'll pee later.
INES. Why don't you play some music from the little radio? If we get an American station we'll know we're moving north.
PEPE. *(Switches on the radio.)* No American stations.
INES. See, who knows where we're heading, we can't even get a northern station! You're not a seaman and neither is he and I don't know anything about the sea, except it's a good place to cry.
JULIO. Give me a cigarette, Pepe. It's going to be a long night.
INES. Give me one, too. Being in the middle of nowhere makes us nervous. Not enough room to walk. Not enough space to run. I know I won't be able to sleep tonight.
JULIO. Me neither.
PEPE. That makes three of us. I have a hard time sleeping on land.
INES. You can't find a damn station?
JULIO. No.
INES. I want to hear an American song to make me feel we're get-

ting closer. Billie Holiday, so I can a have good cry and calm myself. Don't get mad at me, Julio. I feel like crying. *(A Cuban bolero plays, maybe "Lagrimas negras."* She moves to the rhythm.)*
Leave that station on ... Paranh ... pan ... pan ... pan ... panh ...
JULIO. Don't sing. Control yourself. You're making the raft move.
INES. Let me sing ... I feel like singing ... *(She does. The men join in. Ines gets a spoon and makes music with a metal cup. Pepe uses the wood on the raft as a drum. The sound of the ocean swells as the lights dim. The sound of the waves drowns all music. Silence. Lights change.)*

Scene 2

Projected on the screen: SECOND DAY OUT AT SEA. Ines coughs. Julio holds a bottle of water. Pepe is asleep.

JULIO. Drink some water.
INES. This thirst is getting to me. My mouth fills up with a bitter foam.
JULIO. Have some more water. *(She takes another drink.)*
INES. That's enough. I was having a bad dream. I was thirsty as a dry lake and my left breast was overflowing with water. But I couldn't drink, because I couldn't bring my mouth close enough to my chest. But you came close to me and suck the water from my breast and gave me some water to drink. And I couldn't stop drinking from your mouth from my breast, because the thirst was insatiable. I drank and drank water. The more I drank the more water flowed out my breast. And I couldn't stop and neither could you. If you stopped giving me water, the flow would stop. And it felt like I had enough to quench a desert. Just thinking about it gives me a strange sensation, as if I had water in there. *(Brings her hand to her breast.)*
JULIO. Come here ... *(She moves close to him.)* Closer ... Closer ... *(She squats over his legs. He starts unbuttoning her dress.)*
INES. What are you doing?
JULIO. Shshshh ... I want to see your breasts.
INES. Here Julio, in the middle of the sea with Pepe next to us!

* See Special Note on Songs and Recordings on copyright page.

JULIO. Yes ... *(Pulls her close to him. He starts kissing her breasts and her neck.)*
INES. No. You're insane.
JULIO. Why? Come here. I need to drink from you.
INES. But it was a dream.
JULIO. *(He is unzipping his fly.)* Dreams become real.
INES. No. Stop it.
JULIO. Why not? I want to taste you.
INES. We'll wake him up.
JULIO. Stay like this on top of me. We don't have to move, the sea is already moving. Stay like that, like that.
INES. No, Julio.
JULIO. *(Kisses her.)* Yes, stay there.
INES. We'll wake him up. *(She starts giving in.)*
JULIO. No, this could be the last time.
INES. Don't say that!
JULIO. Yes. What if we never make it, my love?
INES. We'll make it.
JULIO. Stay like this as if it were the last time.
INES. We'll make it. Don't say we won't make it.
JULIO. If we don't make it, we can say we did it one last time. I was inside you one last time. One last time.
INES. Why are you so stubborn!
JULIO. Because you make me stubborn. Your skin, your face, having you so close to me, knowing that at any moment life could end for me.
INES. No, not for you. Nothing will happen to you while I'm here. Even if death comes near us I would let it take me first.
JULIO. *(As if reaching an orgasm.)* Oh, Ines ... Ines ... Ines ...
INES. Ay, Julio! *(He lies back.)*
JULIO. You see there was water inside you, like rain. *(She embraces him. They lie back on the raft. The sound of the sea fills the stage. Lights change.)*

Scene 3

Projected on the screen: THIRD DAY OUT AT SEA. Julio and Ines are asleep. Pepe speaks to the sea. He's on top of the sail, looking out at the distance. He is hallucinating.

PEPE. If your voice is coming from there, say something! *(Pause.)* If your voice is coming from there, say something! *(Pause.)* Push me! Push me, like you said you would. *(Sound of children laughing: a distant angelic aria. Then the continual sound of the rippling waves.)* Don't think you can play with my mind! You can't trick me. You're not going to make me lose my head. I'm not sentimental. I'm not. I'm like a fish. Scales. Sharp bones. You never see a fish cry. Why cry when fish live in the water. If I cry, I'll cry in the shower, enh! So no one can see my tears. Tears to the water. Water to the sea. *(Sound of roaring sea. The sound of a child calling someone in the distance. Then it all subsides.)* I've heard what the ocean does to people. I've heard. Like the desert. A fever. You see things. A mirage. You play tricks on the eyes.
    What ever became of that day, eh? What ever became of that day when I was a child, and my father brought the whole family together and said, "We're moving to the coast, and I'm going to show you the sea." And we sold all the chickens to buy the bus fare. We sold the cows and the pigs to rent a house close to the seashore.
    Look ... Look ... You can't trick me! I can close my eyes ... I can close my eyes and see you like that first day, when the driver said, "We're in Havana. We're by the seawall." And I climbed down from the bus, with my eyes closed, and my father said, "Open your eyes, Pepe. Open your eyes. This is the sea. This is the sea." And when I saw you, you were blue and big as the falling sky. Calm and full as a bowl of blue soup ... You were all I imagined you to be.
    Look ... Look ... Look at me running to you. *(Starts running in place.)* Look at me running to drink you! Look! Look!
    You can't trick me! *(Sound of children laughing.)* You can't trick me! You're not a lie! You're not a lie! You're not a lie! You're not a lie! Look at me swimming! Look at me swimming! Look at me

walking on your water — like Jesus. Julio! Ines! I'm walking on top of the sea like Jesus! *(Sound of a woman laughing in the distance. Julio and Ines wake up.)*
JULIO. One can't even ... *(Pepe continues running in place.)*
PEPE. I'm walking ...
INES. Pepe, what's gotten into you!
PEPE. I'm walking ... I'm walking on top of the sea like Jesus.
INES. Stop that Pepe! He's hallucinating, Julio! Grab him! Stop it! Stop! You're going to turn over the raft. *(She tries to make him stop. She tries to pull him down. Sound of children laughing in the distance.)*
PEPE. I'm walking! I'm getting there!
INES. Stop it!
JULIO. Stop it, Pepe! Stop it! STOP! *(Silence. Pepe is transfixed.)*
PEPE. I'm thirsty.
INES. I am, too. Are you all right?
PEPE. My mind ... I ... I thought ...
INES. Yes, Pepe ...
PEPE. I saw things ... The sea ... I thought ... I thought ... My mind ... It left me ... *(Sound of loud thunder. Lights change.)*

FUEGO

FIRE IN THE SEA

Scene 4

Projected on the screen: FOURTH DAY OUT AT SEA. Sunset. Orange lights. Each character in his own world. Spotlight on Julio looking at the sea. He holds a metal cup and is peeing into the cup. The sound of bongo drums.

JULIO. Nothing but water and no water to drink ...
    I'm in the fuckin' middle of nowhere ... I must think of cities and streets, fountains of sweet water ...
    I'm starting to smell like codfish ... sardines ... No, mustn't try to think of those things ... *(Closes his eyes.)*
    It's raining inside me and the rain flows downwards from the mountains, to the valleys ... And the water is so pure that women wash their hair and let their children bathe ... *(Julio takes a swig of urine.)*
PEPE. *(Spotlight on Pepe looking up at the sky.)* If I close my eyes ... If I empty my mind and calm myself maybe sleep will come. Maybe sleep will come ... I'm in the middle of nowhere ...
INES. *(Spotlight on Ines. She is looking at the sea.)* No, mustn't have bad thoughts.
    I always wanted to leave. Always wanted to go ... Now I have in front of me, the sea ... The sea ... I finally got to go ... *(The spotlights fade; dim orange light washes the stage.)*
JULIO. If I close my eyes ...
PEPE. If I calm myself ...
INES. If I think of nothing ...
JULIO. If I think of land, sweet water.
PEPE. I have to tell myself ...
JULIO. Land ...

PEPE. ... that is all a dream ...
INES. Maybe sleep will come ...
JULIO. Maybe sleep will come ...
INES. It will come.
PEPE. I have to tell myself ...
INES. I have to tell myself ...
JULIO. I have to tell myself ...
INES. The sea is my hammock, my hammock ...
JULIO. *(Abruptly.)* We're in the fuckin' middle of nowhere! How the hell did we get into all this rice and mangoes? *(The drums stop. Full lights.)*
INES. *(Hallucinating.)* Somebody is waving at me.
JULIO. Who?
INES. There ...
PEPE. Wave back ... *(In a loud voice.)* Hello!
INES. Hello ...
JULIO. There's nobody there ... It's the sea ... Just the sea ...
INES. It's not the sea ... Somebody is waving at me ...
JULIO. Nothing but water. It's our minds ...
PEPE. Our minds? ... Your mind ... Not my mind ... I like my mind ...
INES. *(In a loud voice.)* — Hello out there! *(Waving. Opens an umbrella. She squints as she looks into the distance.)* Hello out there ... Hello ...
JULIO. *(After a pause.)* See ... No answer ...
INES. What's the matter, you're jealous? Hello, out there!
PEPE. It's not a man it's a woman ...
JULIO. There's nobody out there, get that straight.
   Let's go to sleep, it's getting dark. When morning comes ... When the sun rises ... It will all be blue again ...
PEPE. And we'll see rooftops at last ...
INES. Windows ...
JULIO. Windows she says! We're in the middle of nowhere.
INES. A sewing machine ... When the wind blows gently I hear a sewing machine ...
JULIO. She keeps seeing gondolas and sewing machines ...
PEPE. Are you sure it's not a train? I keep hearing a train.
JULIO. She said a sewing machine, and now you —
PEPE. Then somebody is out there sewing ...
JULIO. *(Looks at Pepe in disbelief.)* Oh God.
INES. Yes, sewing, sewing, Julio ...

JULIO. Sewing what?
PEPE. Handkerchiefs ... White handkerchiefs to wave at us ... Somebody is out there waiting for us ...
JULIO. *(Gives up on the whole thing.)* I'm going to sleep.
INES. I'm still going to keep an eye on my suitcase.
JULIO. What suitcase?
INES. A man took it to the end of the platform ...
JULIO. What platform?
 What's the matter with you! It's the sea ... I keep telling you ... Put this in your head ...
PEPE. *(Trying to explain to her.)* Yes and every time ... What he's saying is that every time ... Every time we see something ...
JULIO. Yes, tell her ...
PEPE. What he's saying is that every time ... Every time we see something ...
JULIO. *(Applauds, waiting to hear something brilliant.)* That's it ... Finally ...
PEPE. *(Puffing himself.)* Every time ... Every time we're getting somewhere, it's just like another time without getting anywhere. Right, Julio? ...
JULIO. Bravo ...
PEPE. *(He turns away and looks at the sky.)* Then one more night to add to the list, till the next night ... Then the moon again ... *(Looking at the moon now.)* Same old glare ... *(Points up.)* One more night with the moon ... And there she is again wearing white gloves, green slippers, reeking of perfume, smoking her cigarette ... And I have to tell her, "Why do you do this to me! ... Why are you dressing up for me! Why are you trying to fool me ... Let me go, enh. Let me go. Just let me be ... " And I have to say, *(In a loud voice. Confused now.)* "Is there anyone out there who knows what's happening!"
JULIO. What is he saying now?
INES. *(Closes her umbrella.)* I don't know what he's saying.
JULIO. What are you saying? What are you saying? Who are you talking to? *(There is a pause. Pepe is still looking at the sky waiting for an answer.)*
INES. He's talking to the moon.
JULIO. He's talking to the moon ... *(To Pepe.)* You better pull yourself together.
PEPE. *(In a vacuum.)* Something has happened, Julio ... You hear? *(Pause.)*

JULIO. Nothing has happened ... Nothing ...
PEPE. Yes something has happened and the world has gone away. There's nobody to talk to ... Nobody to ask.
INES. Ask the man who is waving at me. Julio doesn't like him, but he's still waving at me.
JULIO. There isn't any man and there isn't any moon ...
PEPE. Then we're fucked.
JULIO. You both are scaring the shit out of me ... We're in the middle of nowhere and you're talking nonsense ...
INES. *(Gently.)* When the sun rises, it will be over, Julio.
   I keep seeing a bridge in my dreams. A white bridge, curved like a fallen halo in the middle of the sea.
PEPE. *(Laughs with joy.)* When the sun rises I'll wash and shave my face like before ...
INES. *(Full of joy.)* And I'll walk into my balcony and water my geraniums ... How about you, Julio? *(Julio finds relief and starts to laugh.)*
JULIO. Me ... Oh I wish I could have a cigarette ...
PEPE. *(With an imaginary cigarette.)* Yes, smoke in your mouth, like before. Look at me, smoke in the air taking us back to your house, your table. Opening the windows to let in seven o'clock ...
INES. Ah yes, seven o'clock! That's the time I like to get up. The smell of seven o'clock ... The oleanders by my window ...
PEPE. Coffee ...
INES. Moist leaves ...
JULIO. *(Entering their world.)* Mist ... Bread ...
PEPE. Barbershops ...
INES. Clocks ringing ...
JULIO. Beds being made ... And light making its way under doorways ...
INES. *(Suddenly seeing an imaginary airport.)* You must tell those men to be careful with my suitcase, Julio ... *(To an imaginary person.)* — Be careful. That blue suitcase has never gone anywhere. It's liable to get lost. Doesn't know of farewells and train windows, people waving good-bye ... *(To Pepe and Julio.)* Ay, you don't know how much I wanted a picture sitting on top of my suitcase!
PEPE. I'm thirsty, Julio ... Give me some water ...
JULIO. We don't have any water.
PEPE. You drank it?
JULIO. Me? *(Lost for words.)* We ... You know well ... We didn't have any more ...

PEPE. But there was ... I saw it ... We had ... I saw it with my eyes ... Where's the bottle?
INES. What bottle? *(Pepe starts searching for the bottle. He starts making a mess.)*
PEPE. It was full ...
JULIO. I didn't take any water ...
PEPE. Where is it? Where is it? Where did you hide it?
INES. Where did you see it?
PEPE. I saw it ... It was full.
INES. I didn't drink it.
PEPE. Someone drank it.
JULIO. I didn't drink it.
PEPE. Then who did? Who was it? Give it to me ... You're hiding it ...
I'm not hiding anything ...
PEPE. Give it to me ... *(Grabs him by the shirt.)* You took it. He has it! He has it! Give it to me ... *(Pepe notices he has lost control. He lets go of Julio. He looks down at the waves. Silence. Softly.)* I'm sorry ... I'm ... Something has happened, and I don't know what it is ... I don't know who I am, what to do, what I've done — what's happening, Julio? What's happening? What's happening to me?
JULIO. Calm down.
INES. *(Softly.)* You are Pepe, that's who you are ... And ... And I am Ines ... You are Pepe, and I love you like I love Julio. *(Touches Pepe's face.)* How can you forget who you are? How can you forget?
JULIO. Let's go to sleep. Tomorrow we'll be a little bit closer.
PEPE. Oh God ... Now ... I ... I ... Now ... Now ... Julio, she ... she ... Did you hear what she said?
JULIO. Let's go to sleep ...
INES. But I love ... *(Reaches out to Pepe.)*
JULIO. *(To Ines.)* Leave him alone.
PEPE. *(Looking at Ines.)* Why?
JULIO. Leave him alone.
PEPE. Didn't you hear what she said?
JULIO. Let's go to sleep. We are weak. We are weak and tired, and we don't know what we're doing. We don't know what we're saying.
PEPE. *(Full of joy, he shakes Julio.)* But she says she loves me, Julio. Didn't you hear? *(Moves toward Ines. Pause.)* How can I go to sleep? Why go to sleep, when I feel like shouting! *(Pepe laughs. He touches*

Ines' face. She smiles and kisses his hand. Julio turns in the other direction. Ines lies back on the raft. Pepe admires her beauty. Sound of a large wave. Lights change.)

Scene 5

Projected on the screen: FIFTH DAY OUT AT SEA. Nighttime. Fog. The men are asleep. Ines is awake looking into the distance. She is hallucinating. Sound of a large ship approaching.

INES. Julio, Pepe ... Are you awake? *(Pause.)* I'm going to get ready, you hear. They're out there. They've come for us. You two can stay here sleeping, I'll come back for you ...
   Where's my shawl? *(She starts looking for her shawl.)* What did I do with my shawl? I bought it years ago. I'm going to wear it when we get there. I'm going to run through the seaport with my shawl. Julio, Pepe, can you just see me! You both have to carry me in your arms and lift me up in the air.
   Best to put some powder on. I probably look like a scarecrow. Don't want those people on the ship to see all these long nights on my face ... *(She takes out her compact and starts powdering her face hurriedly. Sound of a large ship approaching.)*
   Eyes red ... Lips dry ... Lucky for this ... Couldn't leave it behind, same compact Mamá used for years ... Just in case I had to see her face in the mirror ...
   Oh, if she could peek from the sky and see that I'm finally getting somewhere! She used to say, Ines, has butterflies in her head.
   Well, you could tell her now: "I'm going to some big land, Mamá!"
   They've come for us! ... And when you have to go you have to go ... Even if I had to leave like a thief, without my traveling shoes, my old blue dress, which I hung in my wardrobe years ago, and my alligator bag ...
   — You both have to hold tight to me when I come back for you. Don't want you falling behind. *(Continues powdering her face.)*
   Morning comes and it's all the same here.

The two of you should've been awake a moment ago, an angel came from heaven and said he was going find us a light bulb to light this part of the sea. You have to light it when he gives it to you. It would make things better, you hear me. That way I can look for your light in the distance. *(Closes her compact. She has powdered her face so much she looks like a clown. She takes out the umbrella. She turns upstage and opens it. A blue glow emanates from the umbrella. She sticks her foot in the water. The lights slowly start to dim.)* I'm just going to make my way to that ship — to that man waving at me. Goodbye, Julio. Goodbye, Pepe ... You just keep your eye on my umbrella, you hear me?

Water is warm, Julio, like a glass of warm milk ... You liked to drink warm milk at night. They say it soothes the mind, like summer rain.

Oh, I can feel the warmth rising to my face. *(The sound of a ship approaching will echo throughout the following section.)* That's a good omen. It's warm like a winter coat, as if a fallen star had bathed in it ... Look at all this blue water, Julio ... Nothing like the sea ... Nothing like the sea ... *(Her voice echoes. Sound of foghorns.)* All these different blues ... Prussian blue, Pompeii blue ... Aquamarine ... Aniline ... Indigo ... *(The lights are fully dimmed. All we see is the glow of the blue umbrella as it moves further and further upstage, away from the boat, and the light from the kerosene lamp on the raft.)* Calamine blue ... Capri blue ... Egyptian blue ... You just keep your eye on my umbrella, you hear me? *(The umbrella is gone.)*
JULIO. *(Waking up.)* Ines ... *(Pause.)* Ines ... Pepe, wake up. Where is Ines? *(Lifts up the kerosene lamp.)* Where did she go? *(Pause.)* Ines. Ines ... Where did she go? Where is she? *(The sound of a large ship fills the space. Lights change.)*

AIRE

Scene 6

Projected on the screen: AIRE. Daytime. Both men are still in a hallucinatory state and are looking out into the distance.

PEPE. Nowhere to be found. She's ...
JULIO. No. Don't say she's gone. She's not gone. She's not gone. Look to your right. She's bound to appear. *(Picks up the compass and throws it.)* Oh, this shit!
PEPE. Julio, you've lost your mind. She's gone ...
JULIO. No. Don't say she's gone. When it's quiet like this ... When it's quiet I can hear her.
PEPE. Me, too.
JULIO. Then don't say she's gone.
PEPE. No, I hear her, too. But I think it's a ghost ... Then you start screaming at me, and we lose her. We see her then we lose her.
JULIO. I won't yell at you anymore. When it's quiet like this ... Do you hear now?
PEPE. No.
JULIO. When it's quiet ... I can hear her so clear.
PEPE. Then it's real. Then she's really with us ...
JULIO. You think so, too?
PEPE. Sure.
JULIO. Then it's her.
PEPE. It's a ghost, Julio.
JULIO. No.
PEPE. Then we have to tell ourselves that we're not seeing things that it's really her.
JULIO. Yes ... Yes ... *(Ines enters singing a song like "Veinte Años."* She holds her umbrella and makes her way to the raft. She sits by Julio.)* Ines ...

---

* See Special Note on Songs and Recordings on copyright page.

INES. Shshhhhh ... You see the blue calamine waves over on that side ... That takes us to a sleepy island where I like to go for tea in the afternoons.
JULIO. *(Looks at Pepe, then at her.)* It's her ... It's you ... I told him ...
INES. Shshhh ... Not too loud ... A woman told me that if I stay here for too long, someone is liable to recognize me ...
JULIO. No. Stay. We won't say anything ... We won't tell.
PEPE. No we won't tell.
INES. She said, "You go on. You just go on ... "
JULIO. She said that! That's good ... We ... We're glad ...
PEPE. We thought ... We thought you had gone ...
JULIO. Don't say it, Pepe ... She's here now ...
INES. Well I said, "I need to get out of this limbo ... What about Julio and Pepe!"
JULIO. You said that?
INES. The woman told me I could sit here and wait for the ship with you ... *(Laughs.)* I said to her it's easier for others to do this ... It's easier for a real person, for a man to do these things, because he can hide his face under a hat ...

I'm not supposed to be here. Someone could recognize me. She said she would get me a red scarf ... *(Becomes excited.)* Can you believe it, me sitting here with you wearing a red scarf? And I said, "Could I possibly be dreaming this?" I mean, if I'm not ... If I'm not ...
JULIO. *(Looks at Pepe.)* No, it's real. It's real like my skin and bones ... You ... You ... You're here ...
PEPE. Sure, it's real ...
JULIO. As long as you don't go anywhere ... And you stay here with us ...
INES. Of course, my love ...

Someone said there's a bus that comes around this time ... We don't want to miss it ...
JULIO. *(Going along with her.)* No, we don't want to miss it.
PEPE. But tell them not to send us any ugly phantoms, like last time ... The ones that took you away ...
JULIO. Pepe, that's enough!
PEPE. They did. They came here on a black bicycle ... They came here and drank all our water and ... and ...
JULIO. It's all right. This morning I was making my bed before I got up, because I had already gotten up in my mind and made the bed ... And I made the bed because we had things to do. We had

to look for you, my love ...
PEPE. Where's the northeast current? That's what we're looking for ...
INES. You must follow the north star, if you want to find the northeast current. But who can trust stars, I've noticed they're like dizzy sailors, who faint and fall into the sea.
JULIO. Then how do we find our way through this mess?
INES. By the blue trains of the sea ... The constant trains crossing the sea ... *(Sound of a distant train.)*
JULIO. I never heard of a train crossing the sea. You mean ... You mean the currents?
INES. There are trains of water sailing everywhere ... *(Sound of a train getting closer.)* Can you hear them? I must go! I must go! The trains ... The trains ... *(Gets up to go.)* I'll try to come back! I'll come back! *(The sound gets louder.)*
JULIO. Wait ... Wait ... Don't go ... You can't go ... *(The sounds fade. Silence.)*
INES. Soon ... Very soon ... Any minute now trees and flowers will surround you again. I know so ... I must go now.
PEPE. The water ... The water ... It's getting shallow around here, Julio ...
INES. *(Starts looking for her shawl.)* Oh Julio, where's my shawl? What did I do with my shawl ... I'm going to get to wear it when we get there ... I'm going to run through the seaport with my shawl ... *(Julio helps her look for the shawl. He finds a cloth bag.)*
JULIO. Could it be here? What's in here? *(Julio hands her the bag.)*
INES. *(Opens it and pulls out the pillowcases.)* I brought those. Didn't want to leave them behind. Take one for you and one for you, Pepe ...
PEPE. What is this for?
INES. I invented this game ... Put it over your head, Julio ... Show Pepe, how to do it ... *(Julio takes a pillowcase and puts it over his head. Pepe lets Ines cover his head as well. She looks at the two of them, then looks into the distance.)*

Soon it will be over. Look at our night almost coming to an end, just like everything else.

That's what I'll miss Julio, seeing the morning get dressed before my eyes — how she pulls her clothes from the sea.

Well, what can I do? I move on. That's one thing I learned from the sea ...
JULIO. Ines ...

INES. Yes ... I move on, Julio ... When you lift up the pillowcase, you'll begin a new life ... *(Music plays. She opens her umbrella and walks away. She disappears. Both men remain with their faces covered. The white screen opens to reveal a green landscape. The men uncover their faces. Blackout.)*

End of Play

PROPERTY LIST

Wooden board (JULIO)
Rope (JULIO)
Pencil and paper (INES)
Wheelchair (JULIO)
Gold chain (JULIO)
Bicycle with bell (PEPE)
Mailbag with mail, including postcard from Venice and letters (PEPE)
Cigarettes and matches (JULIO)
Italian sewing book (PEPE)
Bundle of clothes wrapped in a white tablecloth (INES)
Radio (PEPE)
Sheet (INES)
Photo album (INES)
Scissors (INES)
Pack of French cigarettes (PEPE)
Mirror (JULIO)
Trunk (JULIO)
Lamp with painted lampshade (JULIO)
Silver pot (JULIO)
Package with radio (INES)
Bottle of rum (INES)
3 glasses (INES)
Folded sheets and pillowcases (INES)
Pillowcase and needle and thread (INES)
Raft (INES, PEPE, JULIO)
Oars (INES, PEPE)
Compass (JULIO)
Spoon (INES)
Metal cup (INES, JULIO)
Bottle of water (JULIO)
Umbrella (INES)
Compact (INES)
Kerosene lamp (INES)
Cloth bag (JULIO)

SOUND EFFECTS

Music on radio
Rain and thunder
Swelling sea
Wind and sea
Children laughing
Distant angelic aria
Rippling waves
Roaring sea
Child calling someone in the distance
Woman laughing in the distance
Loud thunder
Bongo drums
Large wave
Large ship approaching
Foghorn
Distant train

NEW PLAYS

★ **MONTHS ON END by Craig Pospisil.** In comic scenes, one for each month of the year, we follow the intertwined worlds of a circle of friends and family whose lives are poised between happiness and heartbreak. "…a triumph…these twelve vignettes all form crucial pieces in the eternal puzzle known as human relationships, an area in which the playwright displays an assured knowledge that spans deep sorrow to unbounded happiness." –*Ann Arbor News*. "…rings with emotional truth, humor…[an] endearing contemplation on love…entertaining and satisfying." –*Oakland Press*. [5M, 5W] ISBN: 0-8222-1892-5

★ **GOOD THING by Jessica Goldberg.** Brings us into the households of John and Nancy Roy, forty-something high-school guidance counselors whose marriage has been increasingly on the rocks and Dean and Mary, recent graduates struggling to make their way in life. "…a blend of gritty social drama, poetic humor and unsubtle existential contemplation…" –*Variety*. [3M, 3W] ISBN: 0-8222-1869-0

★ **THE DEAD EYE BOY by Angus MacLachlan.** Having fallen in love at their Narcotics Anonymous meeting, Billy and Shirley-Diane are striving to overcome the past together. But their relationship is complicated by the presence of Sorin, Shirley-Diane's fourteen-year-old son, a damaged reminder of her dark past. "…a grim, insightful portrait of an unmoored family…" –*NY Times*. "MacLachlan's play isn't for the squeamish, but then, tragic stories delivered at such an unrelenting fever pitch rarely are." –*Variety*. [1M, 1W, 1 boy] ISBN: 0-8222-1844-5

★ **[SIC] by Melissa James Gibson.** In adjacent apartments three young, ambitious neighbors come together to discuss, flirt, argue, share their dreams and plan their futures with unequal degrees of deep hopefulness and abject despair. "A work…concerned with the sound and power of language…" –*NY Times*. "…a wonderfully original take on urban friendship and the comedy of manners—a *Design for Living* for our times…" –*NY Observer*. [3M, 2W] ISBN: 0-8222-1872-0

★ **LOOKING FOR NORMAL by Jane Anderson.** Roy and Irma's twenty-five-year marriage is thrown into turmoil when Roy confesses that he is actually a woman trapped in a man's body, forcing the couple to wrestle with the meaning of their marriage and the delicate dynamics of family. "Jane Anderson's bittersweet transgender domestic comedy-drama …is thoughtful and touching and full of wit and wisdom. A real audience pleaser." –*Hollywood Reporter*. [5M, 4W] ISBN: 0-8222-1857-7

★ **ENDPAPERS by Thomas McCormack.** The regal Joshua Maynard, the old and ailing head of a mid-sized, family-owned book-publishing house in New York City, must name a successor. One faction in the house backs a smart, "pragmatic" man, the other faction a smart, "sensitive" editor and both factions fear what the other's man could do to this house— and to them. "If Kaufman and Hart had undertaken a comedy about the publishing business, they might have written *Endpapers*…a breathlessly fast, funny, and thoughtful comedy …keeps you amused, guessing, and often surprised…profound in its empathy for the paradoxes of human nature." –*NY Magazine*. [7M, 4W] ISBN: 0-8222-1908-5

★ **THE PAVILION by Craig Wright.** By turns poetic and comic, romantic and philosophical, this play asks old lovers to face the consequences of difficult choices made long ago. "The script's greatest strength lies in the genuineness of its feeling." –*Houston Chronicle*. "Wright's perceptive, gently witty writing makes this familiar situation fresh and thoroughly involving." –*Philadelphia Inquirer*. [2M, 1W (flexible casting)] ISBN: 0-8222-1898-4

DRAMATISTS PLAY SERVICE, INC.
440 Park Avenue South, New York, NY 10016   212-683-8960   Fax 212-213-1539
postmaster@dramatists.com   www.dramatists.com

NEW PLAYS

★ **BE AGGRESSIVE by Annie Weisman.** Vista Del Sol is paradise, sandy beaches, avocado-lined streets. But for seventeen-year-old cheerleader Laura, everything changes when her mother is killed in a car crash, and she embarks on a journey to the Spirit Institute of the South where she can learn "cheer" with Bible belt intensity. "...filled with lingual gymnastics...stylized rapid-fire dialogue..." *–Variety.* "...a new, exciting, and unique voice in the American theatre..." *–BackStage West.* [1M, 4W, extras] ISBN: 0-8222-1894-1

★ **FOUR by Christopher Shinn.** Four people struggle desperately to connect in this quiet, sophisticated, moving drama. "...smart, broken-hearted...Mr. Shinn has a precocious and forgiving sense of how power shifts in the game of sexual pursuit...He promises to be a playwright to reckon with..." *–NY Times.* "A voice emerges from an American place. It's got humor, sadness and a fresh and touching rhythm that tell of the loneliness and secrets of life...[a] poetic, haunting play." *–NY Post.* [3M, 1W] ISBN: 0-8222-1850-X

★ **WONDER OF THE WORLD by David Lindsay-Abaire.** A madcap picaresque involving Niagara Falls, a lonely tour-boat captain, a pair of bickering private detectives and a husband's dirty little secret. "Exceedingly whimsical and playfully wicked. Winning and genial. A top-drawer production." *–NY Times.* "Full frontal lunacy is on display. A most assuredly fresh and hilarious tragicomedy of marital discord run amok...absolutely hysterical..." *–Variety.* [3M, 4W (doubling)] ISBN: 0-8222-1863-1

★ **QED by Peter Parnell.** Nobel Prize-winning physicist and all-around genius Richard Feynman holds forth with captivating wit and wisdom in this fascinating biographical play that originally starred Alan Alda. "QED is a seductive mix of science, human affections, moral courage, and comic eccentricity. It reflects on, among other things, death, the absence of God, travel to an unexplored country, the pleasures of drumming, and the need to know and understand." *–NY Magazine.* "Its rhythms correspond to the way that people—even geniuses—approach and avoid highly emotional issues, and it portrays Feynman with affection and awe." *–The New Yorker.* [1M, 1W] ISBN: 0-8222-1924-7

★ **UNWRAP YOUR CANDY by Doug Wright.** Alternately chilling and hilarious, this deliciously macabre collection of four bedtime tales for adults is guaranteed to keep you awake for nights on end. "Engaging and intellectually satisfying...a treat to watch." *–NY Times.* "Fiendishly clever. Mordantly funny and chilling. Doug Wright teases, freezes and zaps us." *–Village Voice.* "Four bite-size plays that bite back." *–Variety.* [flexible casting] ISBN: 0-8222-1871-2

★ **FURTHER THAN THE FURTHEST THING by Zinnie Harris.** On a remote island in the middle of the Atlantic secrets are buried. When the outside world comes calling, the islanders find their world blown apart from the inside as well as beyond. "Harris winningly produces an intimate and poetic, as well as political, family saga." *–Independent (London).* "Harris' enthralling adventure of a play marks a departure from stale, well-furrowed theatrical terrain." *–Evening Standard (London).* [3M, 2W] ISBN: 0-8222-1874-7

★ **THE DESIGNATED MOURNER by Wallace Shawn.** The story of three people living in a country where what sort of books people like to read and how they choose to amuse themselves becomes both firmly personal and unexpectedly entangled with questions of survival. "This is a playwright who does not just tell you what it is like to be arrested at night by goons or to fall morally apart and become an aimless yet weirdly contented ghost yourself. He has the originality to make you feel it." *–Times (London).* "A fascinating play with beautiful passages of writing..." *–Variety.* [2M, 1W] ISBN: 0-8222-1848-8

DRAMATISTS PLAY SERVICE, INC.
440 Park Avenue South, New York, NY 10016   212-683-8960   Fax 212-213-1539
postmaster@dramatists.com   www.dramatists.com

NEW PLAYS

★ **SHEL'S SHORTS by Shel Silverstein.** Lauded poet, songwriter and author of children's books, the incomparable Shel Silverstein's short plays are deeply infused with the same wicked sense of humor that made him famous. "…[a] childlike honesty and twisted sense of humor." *–Boston Herald.* "…terse dialogue and an absurdity laced with a tang of dread give [*Shel's Shorts*] more than a trace of Samuel Beckett's comic existentialism." *–Boston Phoenix.* [flexible casting] ISBN: 0-8222-1897-6

★ **AN ADULT EVENING OF SHEL SILVERSTEIN by Shel Silverstein.** Welcome to the darkly comic world of Shel Silverstein, a world where nothing is as it seems and where the most innocent conversation can turn menacing in an instant. These ten imaginative plays vary widely in content, but the style is unmistakable. "…[*An Adult Evening*] shows off Silverstein's virtuosic gift for wordplay…[and] sends the audience out…with a clear appreciation of human nature as perverse and laughable." *–NY Times.* [flexible casting] ISBN: 0-8222-1873-9

★ **WHERE'S MY MONEY? by John Patrick Shanley.** A caustic and sardonic vivisection of the institution of marriage, laced with the author's inimitable razor-sharp wit. "…Shanley's gift for acid-laced one-liners and emotionally tumescent exchanges is certainly potent…" *–Variety.* "…lively, smart, occasionally scary and rich in reverse wisdom." *–NY Times.* [3M, 3W] ISBN: 0-8222-1865-8

★ **A FEW STOUT INDIVIDUALS by John Guare.** A wonderfully screwy comedy-drama that figures Ulysses S. Grant in the throes of writing his memoirs, surrounded by a cast of fantastical characters, including the Emperor and Empress of Japan, the opera star Adelina Patti and Mark Twain. "Guare's smarts, passion and creativity skyrocket to awesome heights…" *–Star Ledger.* "…precisely the kind of good new play that you might call an everyday miracle…every minute of it is fresh and newly alive…" *–Village Voice.* [10M, 3W] ISBN: 0-8222-1907-7

★ **BREATH, BOOM by Kia Corthron.** A look at fourteen years in the life of Prix, a Bronx native, from her ruthless girl-gang leadership at sixteen through her coming to maturity at thirty. "…vivid world, believable and eye-opening, a place worthy of a dramatic visit, where no one would want to live but many have to." *–NY Times.* "…rich with humor, terse vernacular strength and gritty detail…" *–Variety.* [1M, 9W] ISBN: 0-8222-1849-6

★ **THE LATE HENRY MOSS by Sam Shepard.** Two antagonistic brothers, Ray and Earl, are brought together after their father, Henry Moss, is found dead in his seedy New Mexico home in this classic Shepard tale. "…His singular gift has been for building mysteries out of the ordinary ingredients of American family life…" *–NY Times.* "…rich moments …Shepard finds gold." *–LA Times.* [7M, 1W] ISBN: 0-8222-1858-5

★ **THE CARPETBAGGER'S CHILDREN by Horton Foote.** One family's history spanning from the Civil War to WWII is recounted by three sisters in evocative, intertwining monologues. "…bittersweet music—[a] rhapsody of ambivalence…in its modest, garrulous way…theatrically daring." *–The New Yorker.* [3W] ISBN: 0-8222-1843-7

★ **THE NINA VARIATIONS by Steven Dietz.** In this funny, fierce and heartbreaking homage to *The Seagull*, Dietz puts Chekhov's star-crossed lovers in a room and doesn't let them out. "A perfect little jewel of a play…" *–Shepherdstown Chronicle.* "…a delightful revelation of a writer at play; and also an odd, haunting, moving theater piece of lingering beauty." *–Eastside Journal (Seattle).* [1M, 1W (flexible casting)] ISBN: 0-8222-1891-7

DRAMATISTS PLAY SERVICE, INC.
440 Park Avenue South, New York, NY 10016 212-683-8960 Fax 212-213-1539
postmaster@dramatists.com www.dramatists.com